Color Your Way to a Life You Love™

LET GO

A SELF-HELP ADULT COLORING BOOK FOR RELAXATION & PERSONAL GROWTH!

60 CALMING DESIGNS TO COLOR!
FLOWERS & NATURE
ANIMALS
MANDALAS
DOODLES & PATTERNS

COLOR YOUR WAY TO A LIFE YOU LOVE™: LET GO

For information:
shellijohnson.com
alphadollmedia.com

Copyright Notice and Disclaimers

This book is Copyright © 2018 Shelli Johnson (the "Author"). All Rights Reserved. Published in the United States of America. The legal notices, disclosures, and disclaimers within this book are copyrighted by the Internet Attorneys Association LLC and licensed for use by the Author in this book. All rights reserved.

No part of this book may be reproduced or transmitted in any form or by any means, electronic or mechanical, including photocopying, recording, or by an information storage and retrieval system — except by a reviewer who may quote brief passages in a review to be printed in a magazine, newspaper, blog, or website — without permission in writing from the Author. For information, please contact the Author at the following website address: shellijohnson.com/contact

For more information, please read the "Disclosures and Disclaimers" section at the end of this book.

First Paperback Print Edition, October 2018

Published by Alpha Doll Media, LLC (the "Publisher").

ISBN: 978-0-9747109-4-5

WELCOME TO THE
COLOR YOUR WAY TO A LIFE YOU LOVE™
COLORING BOOK SERIES!

AVAILABLE NOW OR COMING SOON!

UNLEASH YOUR INNER CREATOR & MAKE IT YOUR OWN!

This is not just another coloring book, it's also an invitation for you to delve deeper into who you are so you can find out what makes you come alive. I'm a big believer in the power of taking small steps to get you anywhere you need or want to go. With that in mind, I invite you inside these pages on a creative self-help adventure. You'll unleash your artistic side with designs and patterns while you do daily small-sized activities aimed at: 1. helping you heal yourself and 2. inspiring you to create a life you love. My hope is that you'll use these pages to ignite your imagination, discard your limitations, and free your inner creator.

Feel free to add your own personal embellishments to any image. You can make each page as unique as you like by adding doodles, patterns, and/or shapes. Color the images any way you like with any tools you like. There are no rules except that you relax, enjoy, and color in a way that feels right to you.

THE MEANING & PURPOSE OF LIFE!

"The meaning of life is to find your gift. The purpose of life is to give it away."
—Pablo Picasso

THE PSYCHOLOGY OF COLOR!

From my layman's understanding of the meaning of colors, certain colors can evoke certain emotions.

BLUE: centered, calm, hopeful, confidence
GREEN: growth, safety, endurance, calm
ORANGE: energy, happiness, encouragement, excitement
RED: passion, energy, strength, power, determination
YELLOW: joy, energy, cheerfulness
BROWN: stability
PURPLE: power, ambition, creativity, energy
BLACK: power, elegance, mystery
WHITE: light, goodness, safety

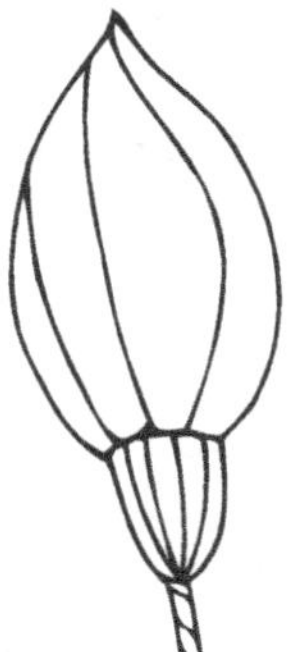

So keep that in mind as you color. If you're looking to experience a particular emotion/feeling/mood, you may want to use a particular color to help you get there.

A FEW HELPFUL SUGGESTIONS!

BABY STEPS
I'm a big believer in the power of taking baby steps to get you anywhere you need or want to go, which is why this coloring book is written the way it is. Each day has small-sized activities. They build on each other, one to the next. So feel free to color whichever image you'd like, just know you'll be best served to do the daily activities in order.

NO PERFECTION NEEDED
Do yourself a kindness and make a mistake in this coloring book early on. Scribble on some of the pages. Spill your favorite beverage on the cover. Rip one of the corners off. Color outside the lines. Make this book imperfect so that you'll feel free to be your real, honest self inside the pages. Being real, not being perfect, is what's going to heal you and set you free.

BE HONEST
I'd recommend that you don't show your answers inside this coloring book to anyone. Keep them to yourself for right now until you make it all the way through Day 30. Why? Honesty with yourself is what's going to help you heal and grow. You won't be completely honest if you're worried about someone reading your answers. In fact, what you're likely to do is tweak your responses, edit them, or scratch them out entirely if you're worried about how others might perceive you. So be kind to yourself & let this coloring book be just for you.

BE WILLING & OPEN
The first step to change is to be open & willing to it. You picked up this coloring book because you're struggling in this area of your life. If you want things to be different, well, both you & those things are going to have to change. So be open to experiencing something new & be willing to do the effort to get there.

GIVE YOURSELF PERMISSION
It's hugely important to give yourself permission (whether that's verbally or written) to: do the daily steps in this book, be/have/do/say/believe whatever you need to so that you can heal yourself, give yourself unlimited tries as many times as it takes, believe in your own worth and value, choose to create a life you love because you matter. Whenever you feel like you need someone else's permission to make a choice about your life, you just give that permission to yourself. The only permission you ever need to live your own life is your own.

YOU'RE ON A JOURNEY
It doesn't matter how old you are, how many times you've tried, or how far there is left to go. It's never too late to be the person you want to be. It's okay if you don't know things yet. You're on a journey and you'll figure it out as you go. This coloring book is designed to help you do just that.

BEGIN YOUR DAY WITH A STEP
If at all possible, do your daily step shortly after you wake up. That way, you'll be able to focus on yourself (because you're absolutely worth the time to do that) before your day gets away from you. So grab your favorite beverage. Find a quiet place. Relax and reflect while you're being creative.

IT'S A PRACTICE & A PROCESS
There's no doing this perfectly, and that's okay. You strive for progress. You do the best you can. So show yourself some patience and kindness because self-compassion is what you most need to heal yourself. You will make mistakes, there's just no way around it. Don't ever use any mistake as a reason to give up on yourself. Just circle back around and start again. And know this: every mistake is simply a brand new chance to do it better the next time.

AND FINALLY . . .
Remember (not just for this book but for all of life): you get out what you put in. So make yourself a priority in your own life because: 1. you're absolutely worth the effort and 2. no one else can do it for you. And one last suggestion good both for this book and for all of life: be brave and color outside the lines, that's where freedom lies.

THOSE WHO ARE BRAVE ARE FREE!

"It is not the critic who counts; not the man who points out how the strong man stumbles, or where the doer of deeds could have done them better. The credit belongs to the man who is actually in the arena, whose face is marred by dust and sweat and blood; who strives valiantly; who errs, who comes short again and again, because there is no effort without error and shortcoming; but who does actually strive to do the deeds; who knows great enthusiasms, the great devotions; who spends himself in a worthy cause; who at the best knows in the end the triumph of high achievement, and who at the worst, if he fails, at least fails while daring greatly, so that his place shall never be with those cold and timid souls who neither know victory nor defeat."

—Theodore Roosevelt

Source: excerpt (also known as *The Man In The Arena*) from the speech "Citizenship in a Republic" delivered at The Sorbonne in Paris, France on April 23, 1910.

COLOR TEST PAGE

Let go or be dragged.
—Proverb

1
1. Today, relax.
2. Take a deep breath in through your nose.
3. Hold it for three seconds.
4. Let it out through your mouth.
5. Then pull your shoulders down away from your ears.
6. Repeat five times.
7. Massage your temples & the back of your neck.
8. Repeat often, especially every time you feel like you're hanging on tight when you know it's time to let go.

2

1. Today, know that you are not alone.
2. You may feel alone. You may feel like no one else has a problem letting go & moving on while you hold on tight & suffer.
3. But know this: one of the main reasons people stay stuck & don't move forward in their lives is because they're hanging on to something (person/place/thing/idea/belief/etcetera) & they refuse to let it go.
4. So don't be so hard on yourself. Instead, remind yourself that you're not alone, that you are in fact in excellent company with the rest of us who are/have been refusing to let go, as often as needed.

3

1. Today, open yourself up.
2. Make a fist with all your strength, as hard & as tight as you can.
3. Hold it. Feel the stress & tension. Feel the ache & burn.
4. Now open your hand & release that fist.
5. Feel the stress & tension release. Feel the relief.
6. Know this: that's what letting go of things that no longer serve you feels like, both a release & a relief. Know this too: there's no room for anything in a closed fist. The same goes for your life. New people/places/things/etcetera won't fit into your life if you steadfastly refuse to hang on to the old.

4

1. Today, realize the truth.
2. Let go of believing that you'll let go once & never have to let go again.
3. Know this: letting go is a process & a practice. Sometimes you let go fast (once & done!) & other times you let go in stages. It's a practice because you often have to do it over & over. But like anything you practice, it'll get easier & you'll get better at it over time. Know this: change is your friend & letting go voluntarily is much easier on you than being forced to let go.
4. Take a deep breath in through your nose, hold, then let it out your mouth.

5

1. Today, unleash your superpower.
2. Let go of not listening for your intuition.
3. Know this: your intuition, which includes both your body (how it feels/reacts) & mind (that calm small voice), is full of wisdom. It will *never* tear you down or berate you. It'll *always* encourage you, strengthen you, guide you, & help you grow, even if what it's saying you need to do to let go & move on scares you.
4. Be alone, ask yourself questions about your life (like: *What am I being guided to do to move forward in my life?*), get quiet & listen inward, write your answers.

Embrace change. Breathe deeply. Remember: it's a process & a practice.

6

1. Today, be honorable.
2. Let go of not trusting yourself.
3. Answer this honestly: *Would I put my life in the hands of someone I didn't trust?*
4. Know this: your life is already in your hands. It's up to you how you want to live it.
5. Write a list of things you have promised &/or want to promise yourself.
6. Pick one item on that list & do/start it today. Keep your word to yourself *every time*. If you repeatedly keep your word to yourself, the self-trust will come.

Embrace change. Breathe deeply. Remember: it's a process & a practice.

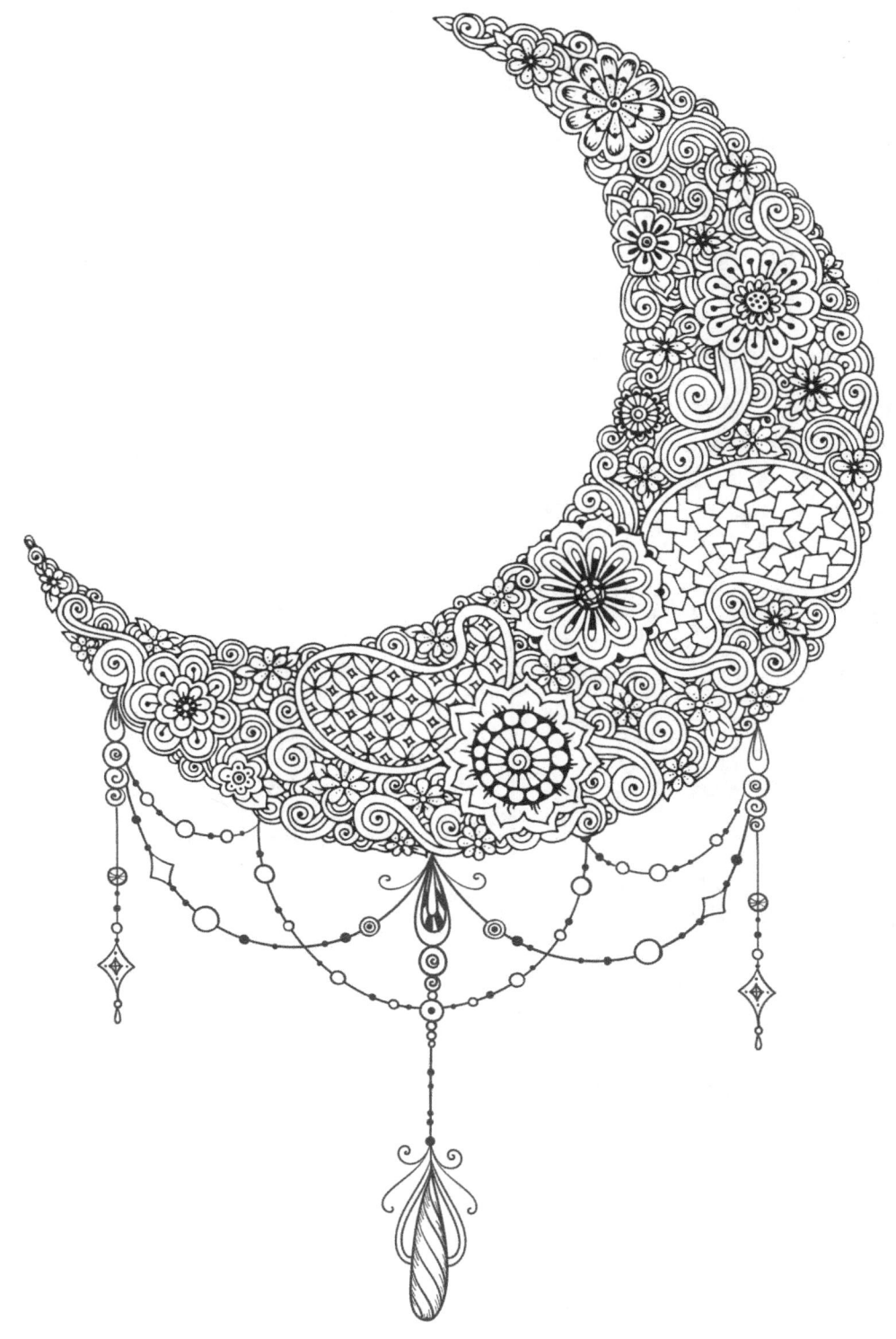

7

1. Today, empower yourself.
2. Be alone for at least 15 minutes & let your intuition guide you & help you move forward in your life. Quickly (so no overthinking or editing) write a list of people/places/things/behaviors/thoughts/etcetera that no longer serve you.
3. Know this: you'll know which things no longer serve you because they hinder you, drain your energy, make you feel less than, don't encourage you, don't aid you in reaching your goals, &/or don't help you create a life you love.
4. This list is all the things that you currently know that you need to let go of.

Embrace change. Breathe deeply. Remember: it's a process & a practice.

8

1. Today, practice self-compassion.
2. Let go of not loving yourself.
3. Today & *every day*, be kind, gentle, & patient with yourself as you learn, grow, & let go. Love yourself because you're the only one of you that there is. Believe in your own worth & value *always*. Say words to encourage yourself. Take excellent care of yourself *every day*.
4. Write today's to-do list. Put your name at the top of that list Answer this: *What would I love to do today just for me?* Go do it, guilt-free. Repeat often.

Embrace change. Breathe deeply. Remember: it's a process & a practice.

9

1. Today, settle in to the in-between.
2. Let go of fear.
3. Know this: the hardest part of letting go is often the unknown. The in-between is that place where you let go of the familiar (& so you think safe) & you venture out into something brand new (where safety is not assured).
4. Write a list of fears about letting go of those things that are familiar to you.
5. Now breathe deeply, practice self-compassion, & let the space between where you are now & where you most want to be motivate you instead of scare you.

Embrace change. Breathe deeply. Remember: it's a process & a practice.

10

1. Today, empower yourself some more.
2. Let go of not acting upon your intuition.
3. Read through your list from Day 7. Pick one, listen for your intuition, & write down what you need to have/be/do/say to let go of that particular item. Breathe deeply & be open to whatever answers come.
4. Now take action based upon those answers & let go, even if that scares you.
5. Remember: let the space between where you are now & where you most want to be motivate you instead of scare you.

Embrace change. Be motivated, not scared. It's a process & a practice.

11

1. Today, open yourself up to possibility.
2. Let go of rigid thinking (especially *always* or *never* thoughts) & resistance.
3. Write a list of things you wish were possible for you, but you believe are not.
4. For each one, write answers to these: *Wouldn't it be cool if something different was possible? Wouldn't it be cool if it was possible for me to actually have/be/do/say that? Wouldn't it be cool if I didn't have to be limited anymore?*
5. Now circle the one that you feel most drawn to. Breathe deeply then take action to make it happen. Make this your belief instead: *I'm possible!*

Embrace change. Be motivated, not scared. It's a process & a practice.

12

1. Today, bring yourself peace.
2. Let go of emotions that don't serve you.
3. Know this: emotions that don't serve you are those that get you crazed/upset (like panic/worry/despair/bitterness/resentment/shame/self-pity/etcetera) but will not change the outcome one bit. They are usually born out of fear.
4. Write a list of emotions that are keeping you from feeling peace. Let yourself *fully* feel them then let them go. Now write actions you can take that'll actually improve your situation. Pick one action & do it to restore your peace.

Embrace change. Be motivated, not scared. It's a process & a practice.

13

1. Today, heal yourself.
2. Let go of thoughts that don't serve you.
3. Know this: thoughts that don't serve you are those that make you feel depressed/defeated/less than/not good enough/self-doubt/distracted/discouraged/etcetera. They don't help you become who you want to be.
4. Refer to your list from Day 7. Add any other thoughts that are hindering you.
5. Then write a list of helpful thoughts that will actually spur you on to improve your life & grow you into the person you envision yourself to be.

Embrace change. Be motivated, not scared. It's a process & a practice.

14

1. Today, heal yourself some more.
2. Let go of beliefs & stories (made from beliefs) that no longer serve you.
3. Know this: you will *always* live out what you believe. Beliefs/stories are just thoughts you've repeated to yourself over & over & over. They can be changed.
4. Read through your list from Day 13. Circle any thoughts that have become beliefs/stories that are now keeping you from creating a life you love. Add any other helpful thoughts that you'd rather believe instead. Now repeat all those helpful thoughts until they become the new beliefs/stories that guide you.

Embrace change. Be motivated, not scared. It's a process & a practice.

15

1. Today, protect yourself.
2. Let go of people that no longer serve you &/or of trying to save others.
3. Know this: people that no longer serve you are those who make you feel small/trapped/negative/incapable/etcetera just by being around &/or thinking of them. This also includes people who want/expect you to fix their lives.
4. Refer to your list from Day 7. Now add the names of any other people who are keeping you from creating a life that matters to you.
5. Do yourself a kindness & limit your time with them or let them go entirely.

Embrace change. Be motivated, not scared. It's a process & a practice.

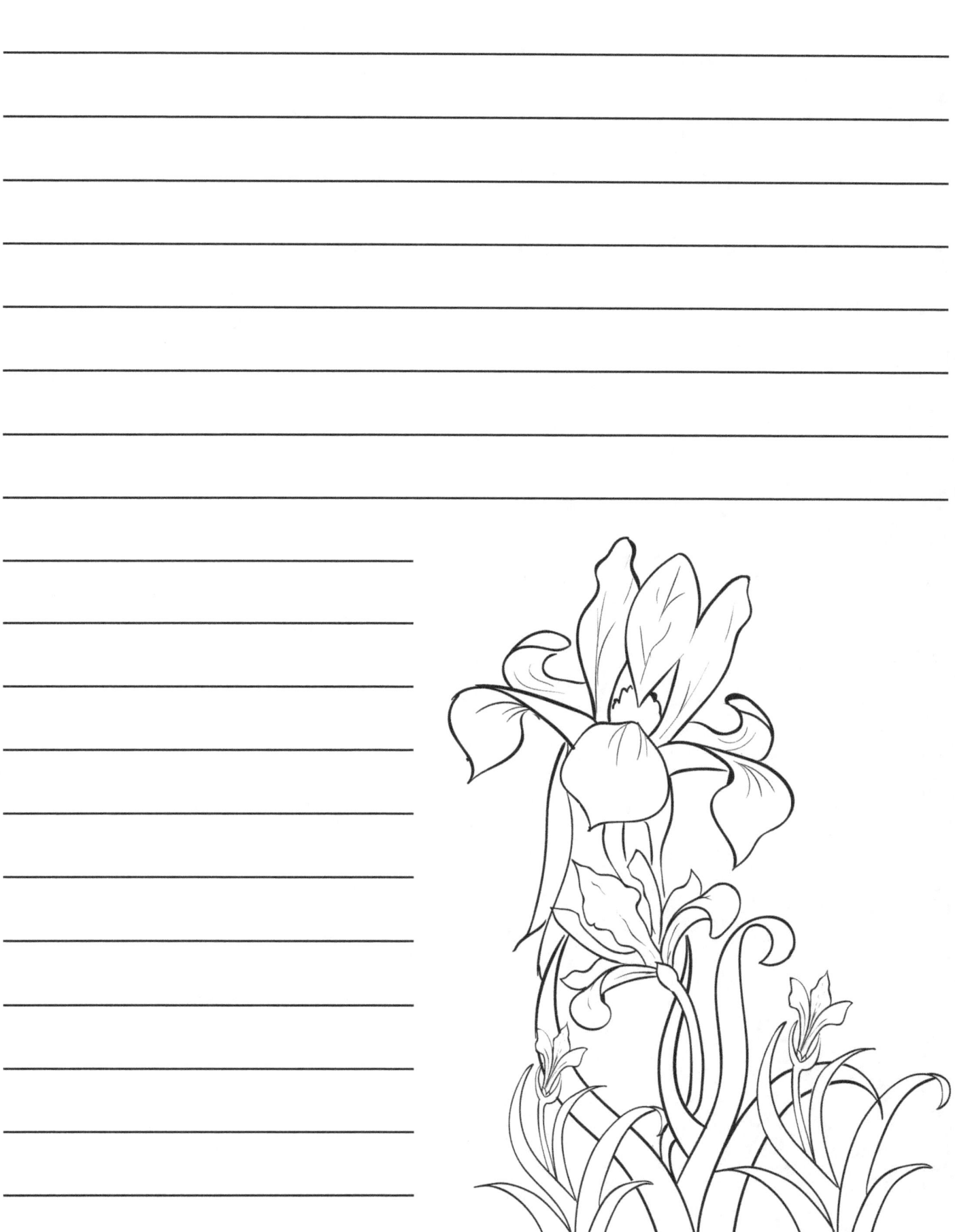

16

1. Today, respect yourself.
2. Let go of behaviors that no longer serve you.
3. Know this: behaviors that no longer serve you are those that harm you physically, mentally, &/or spiritually (including addictions/bad habits/waiting for others to save you/blaming others for your choices/making excuses/etcetera).
4. Refer to your list from Day 7. Add any other behaviors that keep you from being the person you want to be. Now circle the one that does the greatest harm to you & *take action* to free yourself from that behavior today.

Embrace change. Be motivated, not scared. It's a process & a practice.

17

1. Today, honor yourself.
2. Let go of places that no longer serve you.
3. Know this: places that no longer serve you are those that make you feel negative about yourself &/or your life just by being in or near them.
4. Refer to your list from Day 7. Now add the names of any other places that are keeping you from creating a life you love.
5. Do yourself a kindness & limit your time in those places or cut them out of your life entirely. Remember: it's your life that you're working to save.

Embrace change. Be motivated, not scared. It's a process & a practice.

18

1. Today, recognize what you have the power to change & what you don't.
2. Let go of the need to control.
3. Know this: absolute security is an illusion; there are no guarantees of either safety or comfort in nature.
4. Write a list of things you're trying to control, including others & outcomes.
5. Then write a list of choices & actions that are within your power to take.
6. Pick one choice/action & do it today to empower yourself. Repeat often. Choose to stop fighting against what you have no power to change.

Embrace change. Be motivated, not scared. It's a process & a practice.

19

1. Today, stay in the present moment.
2. Let go of past & future events (& the stories you tell yourself about them).
3. Write a list of regrets from your past & worries about your future (what could've/should've/would've been or could/should/might be).
4. Know this: all the regret & worry in the world will never change a thing.
5. For regrets: write down what you can learn from each one. For worries: write what actions you can take *right now* to get you where you want to be.
6. Now start where you are, practice self-compassion, & move forward.

Embrace change. Be motivated, not scared. It's a process & a practice.

20

1. Today, be real.
2. Let go of the fantasy &/or of refusing to accept reality.
3. Write a list of areas in your life where you may be pretending (situations/personal preferences/finances/career/relationships/family/etcetera).
4. For each area, write an answer to this: *How is pretending serving me?*
5. Now write an answer to this: *What actions do I need to take to make my reality a place where I actually want to live?* Then take one action today.
6. Repeat until you reach a life you love, one that is true to you.

Embrace change. Be motivated, not scared. It's a process & a practice.

21

1. Today, build a support system.
2. Let go of doing everything on your own.
3. Write a list of people *whom you trust* to encourage you, support you, &/or help you grow into the person you want & are meant to be.
4. Reach out to one of them today, tell them about what you are letting go, & ask for what you need.
5. Let them be a source of comfort, strength, &/or assistance for you as you embrace change & move forward in your life.

Embrace change. Be motivated, not scared. It's a process & a practice.

22

1. Today, free yourself.
2. Let go of not forgiving yourself.
3. Know this: if you refuse to forgive yourself, you will forever haul around the weight of each & every mistake/failure/weakness/bad choice/etcetera.
4. Write a list of things you refuse to forgive yourself for. For each one ask: *What if I had to experience that so I could learn about myself?* Write what each experience taught you so you can change the story you tell yourself & move forward lighter. Now love yourself enough to give yourself unlimited tries.

Embrace change. Be motivated, not scared. It's a process & a practice.

23

1. Today, free yourself some more.
2. Let go of not forgiving others.
3. Know this: if you refuse to forgive others, you will spend your time & energy attempting to get what you believe you're owed.
4. Write a list of people whom you refuse to forgive.
5. Ask yourself: *Do I really want to spend my life chasing after him/her?*
6. Choose (yes, it's a choice) to release them from their debt to you so you can put your focus back on your own life/hopes/dreams/goals & move on.

Embrace change. Be motivated, not scared. It's a process & a practice.

24

1. Today, stop caring what other people think of you & befriend yourself instead.
2. Let go of comparison, perfectionism, & trying to impress or prove your worth.
3. Know this: comparison is simply an act of self-abuse & perfectionism is based in fear that you are not enough. But you are enough as-is, right now, as you are. Your worth & value are innate; you were born with them, you don't have to do anything to earn them, & nobody can ever take them away from you. So you can be yourself with no need to impress & nothing to prove to anyone.
4. Practice self-compassion as you grow into the person you want to become.

Embrace change. Be motivated, not scared. It's a process & a practice.

25

1. Today, choose abundance.
2. Let go of believing there's not enough for you &/or that it's too late for you.
3. Know this: you will live out what you believe. So choose to believe these: *I get everything I need right when I need it; there is always more than enough for me. It's not too late; I'm still breathing so there's still time.*
4. Remember: you make a belief by simply thinking the same thought over & over. So do yourself a kindness & create beliefs that help you instead of hinder you.
5. Now write a list of at least five things that are good in your life. Repeat often.

Embrace change. Be motivated, not scared. It's a process & a practice.

26

1. Today, become who you've always wanted to be.
2. Let go of anyone else's hopes/wishes/wants/dreams for your life.
3. Write an answer to these: *What if that thing I'm hanging on to so tight wasn't there, would I still be me? What if I was meant to have/be/do something else?*
4. Write a list of things that: you're good at, you love to do, deeply matter to you, make you feel the most alive, &/or you want to achieve during your lifetime.
5. Then with that list as a guide, write a detailed description of what *your* ideal life & *your* idea of success looks like to you.

Embrace change. Be motivated, not scared. It's a process & a practice.

27

1. Today, love your life *now*.
2. Let go of getting in your own way.
3. Make two columns. In the first column, write: WHAT I LOVE. (Refer back to Day 26 for answers.) In the second column, write: WHY I DON'T DO IT.
4. Then answer those & *be honest*. Know this: you most likely aren't doing what you love because of fear. Find the common thread in your answers & you'll discover your biggest fear.
5. Then let go of that fear (see Day 9); choose to be motivated instead of scared.

Embrace change. Be motivated, not scared. It's a process & a practice.

28

1. Today, be brave.
2. Let go of hiding your own light.
3. Read your answers from Days 26 & 27. What you love to do is your light.
4. Know this: hiding your light serves no one, least of all yourself. Happiness lies in building a life around what makes you come alive & fulfills you.
5. Circle the one that matters most to you & do it today. Find time *every day* to do one thing that sparks a light in you because: 1. your happiness is your responsibility & 2. wanting anything for your life is reason enough to pursue it.

Embrace change. Be motivated, not scared. It's a process & a practice.

29

1. Today, step out of your comfort zone.
2. Let go & move on.
3. Know this: you'll never realize your potential by staying stuck in your comfort zone; hanging on to anything that no longer serves you is what keeps you locked inside the limits of that zone. There are things you are meant to have/be/do/say in your lifetime. You won't realize them if you refuse to let go & move on. Remember that when it comes time to make a choice to let go.
4. So ask for help if you need to (see Day 21), & step into the thrilling unknown.

Embrace change. Be motivated, not scared. It's a process & a practice.

30

1. Today, celebrate!
2. Be proud of yourself for how far you've come.
3. Write down your successes & victories (big or small).
4. Do something nice for yourself (like a prize for a job well done).
5. Go & enjoy your life!

Embrace change. Be motivated, not scared. It's a process & a practice.

ABOUT THE AUTHOR!

This book was born out of Shelli Johnson's own struggle to let go. She wanted and needed to heal herself. She wanted and needed practical and easy steps she could take to release those things that were bogging her down so she could move forward. So she simply wrote the book she needed to read. Every day, she does her best to cut herself some slack & practice progress, not perfection.

Shelli's also an award-winning journalist (sports reporting), novelist (grand prize winner), and blogger (shellijohnson.com/blog). She's a truck owner, horse rider, photographer, yoga enthusiast, and slow-cooker fan (shellijohnson.com/recipes). Find out more at: shellijohnson.com/about

Find out about Shelli's other books at:

shellijohnson.com/books

GET YOUR FREE STUFF!

Visit: shellijohnson.com/signup
Opt-in for the newsletter to keep in touch.
Get a free bookmark to color.

ACKNOWLEDGMENTS!

My sincere thanks to people who make my days brighter:
Rollin Johnson
Heather Porazzo

Disclosures and Disclaimers

This book is published in print format. All trademarks and service marks are the properties of their respective owners. All references to these properties are made solely for editorial purposes. Except for marks actually owned by the Author or the Publisher, no commercial claims are made to their use, and neither the Author nor the Publisher is affiliated with such marks in any way.

Unless otherwise expressly noted, none of the individuals or business entities mentioned herein has endorsed the contents of this book.

Limits of Liability & Disclaimers of Warranties

Because this book is a general educational information product, it is not a substitute for professional advice on the topics discussed in it.

The materials in this book are provided "as is" and without warranties of any kind either express or implied. The Author and the Publisher disclaim all warranties, express or implied, including, but not limited to, implied warranties of merchantability and fitness for a particular purpose. The Author and the Publisher do not warrant that defects will be corrected. The Author does not warrant or make any representations regarding the use or the results of the use of the materials in this book in terms of their correctness, accuracy, reliability, or otherwise. Applicable law may not allow the exclusion of implied warranties, so the above exclusion may not apply to you.

Under no circumstances, including, but not limited to, negligence, shall the Author or the Publisher be liable for any special or consequential damages that result from the use of, or the inability to use this book, even if the Author, the Publisher, or an authorized representative has been advised of the possibility of such damages. Applicable law may not allow the limitation or exclusion of liability or incidental or consequential damages, so the above limitation or exclusion may not apply to you. In no event shall the Author or Publisher total liability to you for all damages, losses, and causes of action (whether in contract, tort, including but not limited to, negligence or otherwise) exceed the amount paid by you, if any, for this book.

You agree to hold the Author and the Publisher of this book, principals, agents, affiliates, and employees harmless from any and all liability for all claims for damages due to injuries, including attorney fees and costs, incurred by you or caused to third parties by you, arising out of the products, services, and activities discussed in this book, excepting only claims for gross negligence or intentional tort.

You agree that any and all claims for gross negligence or intentional tort shall be settled solely by confidential binding arbitration per the American Arbitration Association's commercial arbitration rules. Your claim cannot be aggregated with third party claims. All arbitration must occur in the municipality where the Author's principal place of business is located. Arbitration fees and costs shall be split equally, and you are solely responsible for your own lawyer fees.

Facts and information are believed to be accurate at the time they were placed in this book. All data provided in this book is to be used for information purposes only. The information contained within is not intended to provide specific legal, financial, tax, physical or mental health advice, or any other advice whatsoever, for any individual or company and should not be relied upon in that regard. The services described are only offered in jurisdictions where they may be legally offered. Information provided is not all-inclusive, and is limited to information that is made available and such information should not be relied upon as all-inclusive or accurate.

For more information about this policy, please contact the Author at the website address listed in the Copyright Notice at the front of this book.

IF YOU DO NOT AGREE WITH THESE TERMS AND EXPRESS CONDITIONS, DO NOT READ THIS BOOK. YOUR USE OF THIS BOOK, INCLUDING PRODUCTS, SERVICES, AND ANY PARTICIPATION IN ACTIVITIES MENTIONED IN THIS BOOK, MEAN THAT YOU ARE AGREEING TO BE LEGALLY BOUND BY THESE TERMS.

Affiliate Compensation & Material Connections Disclosure

This book may contain references to websites and information created and maintained by other individuals and organizations. The Author and the Publisher do not control or guarantee the accuracy, completeness, relevance, or timeliness of any information or privacy policies posted on these websites.

You should assume that all references to products and services in this book are made because material connections exist between the Author or Publisher and the providers of the mentioned products and services ("Provider"). You should also assume that all website links within this book are affiliate links for (a) the Author, (b) the Publisher, or (c) someone else who is an affiliate for the mentioned products and services (individually and collectively, the "Affiliate").

The Affiliate recommends products and services in this book based in part on a good faith belief that the purchase of such products or services will help readers in general.

The Affiliate has this good faith belief because (a) the Affiliate has tried the product or service mentioned prior to recommending it or (b) the Affiliate has researched the reputation of the Provider and has made the decision to recommend the Provider's products or services based on the Provider's history of providing these or other products or services.

The representations made by the Affiliate about products and services reflect the Affiliate's honest opinion based upon the facts known to the Affiliate at the time this book was published.

Because there is a material connection between the Affiliate and Providers of products or services mentioned in this book, you should always assume that the Affiliate may be biased because of the Affiliate's relationship with a Provider and/or because the Affiliate has received or will receive something of value from a Provider.

Perform your own due diligence before purchasing a product or service mentioned in this book.

The type of compensation received by the Affiliate may vary. In some instances, the Affiliate may receive complimentary products (such as a review copy), services, or money from a Provider prior to mentioning the Provider's products or services in this book.

In addition, the Affiliate may receive a monetary commission or non-monetary compensation when you take action by using a website link within in this book. This includes, but is not limited to, when you purchase a product or service from a Provider after going to a website link contained in this book.

Health Disclaimers

As an express condition to reading to this book, you understand and agree to the following terms.

This book is a general educational health-related information product. This book does not contain medical advice.

The book's content is not a substitute for direct, personal, professional medical care and diagnosis. None of the exercises or treatments (including products and services) mentioned in this book should be performed or otherwise used without prior approval from your physician or other qualified professional health care provider.

There may be risks associated with participating in activities or using products and services mentioned in this book for people in poor health or with pre-existing physical or mental health conditions.

Because these risks exist, you will not use such products or participate in such activities if you are in poor health or have a pre-existing mental or physical condition. If you choose to participate in these risks, you do so of your own free will and accord, knowingly and voluntarily assuming all risks associated with such activities.

Earnings & Income Disclaimers
No Earnings Projections, Promises or Representations

For purposes of these disclaimers, the term "Author" refers individually and collectively to the author of this book and to the affiliate (if any) whose affiliate hyperlinks are referenced in this book.

You recognize and agree that the Author and the Publisher have made no implications, warranties, promises, suggestions, projections, representations or guarantees whatsoever to you about future prospects or earnings, or that you will earn any money, with respect to your purchase of this book, and that the Author and the Publisher have not authorized any such projection, promise, or representation by others.

Any earnings or income statements, or any earnings or income examples, are only estimates of what you might earn. There is no assurance you will do as well as stated in any examples. If you rely upon any figures provided, you must accept the entire risk of not doing as well as the information provided. This applies whether the earnings or income examples are monetary in nature or pertain to advertising credits which may be earned (whether such credits are convertible to cash or not).

There is no assurance that any prior successes or past results as to earnings or income (whether monetary or advertising credits, whether convertible to cash or not) will apply, nor can any prior successes be used, as an indication of your future success or results from any of the information, content, or strategies. Any and all claims or representations as to income or earnings (whether monetary or advertising credits, whether convertible to cash or not) are not to be considered as "average earnings".

Testimonials & Examples

Testimonials and examples in this book are exceptional results, do not reflect the typical purchaser's experience, do not apply to the average person and are not intended to represent or guarantee that anyone will achieve the same or similar results. Where specific income or earnings (whether monetary or advertising credits, whether convertible to cash or not), figures are used and attributed to a specific individual or business, that individual or business has earned that amount. There is no assurance that you will do as well using the same information or strategies. If you rely on the specific income or earnings figures used, you must accept all the risk of not doing as well. The described experiences are atypical. Your financial results are likely to differ from those described in the testimonials.

The Economy

The economy, where you do business, on a national and even worldwide scale, creates additional uncertainty and economic risk. An economic recession or depression might negatively affect your results.

Your Success or Lack of It

Your success in using the information or strategies provided in this book depends on a variety of factors. The Author and the Publisher have no way of knowing how well you will do because they do not know you, your background, your work ethic, your dedication, your motivation, your desire, or your business skills or practices. Therefore, neither the Author nor the Publisher guarantees or implies that you will get rich, that you will do as well, or that you will have any earnings (whether monetary or advertising credits, whether convertible to cash or not), at all.

Businesses and earnings derived therefrom involve unknown risks and are not suitable for everyone. You may not rely on any information presented in this book or otherwise provided by the Author or the Publisher, unless you do so with the knowledge and understanding that you can experience significant losses (including, but not limited to, the loss of any monies paid to purchase this book and/or any monies spent setting up, operating, and/or marketing your business activities, and further, that you may have no earnings at all (whether monetary or advertising credits, whether convertible to cash or not).

Forward-Looking Statements

Materials in this book may contain information that includes or is based upon forward-looking statements within the meaning of the Securities Litigation Reform Act of 1995. Forward-looking statements give the Author's expectations or forecasts of future events. You can identify these statements by the fact that they do not relate strictly to historical or current facts. They use words such as "anticipate," "estimate," "expect," "project," "intend," "plan," "believe," and other words and terms of similar meaning in connection with a description of potential earnings or financial performance.

Any and all forward looking statements here or on any materials in this book are intended to express an opinion of earnings potential. Many factors will be important in determining your actual results and no guarantees are made that you will achieve results similar to the Author or anybody else. In fact, no guarantees are made that you will achieve any results from applying the Author's ideas, strategies, and tactics found in this book.

Purchase Price

Although the Publisher believes the price is fair for the value that you receive, you understand and agree that the purchase price for this book has been arbitrarily set by the Publisher or the vendor who sold you this book. This price bears no relationship to objective standards.

Due Diligence

You are advised to do your own due diligence when it comes to making any decisions. Use caution and seek the advice of qualified professionals before acting upon the contents of this book or any other information. You shall not consider any examples, documents, or other content in this book or otherwise provided by the Author or Publisher to be the equivalent of professional advice.

The Author and the Publisher assume no responsibility for any losses or damages resulting from your use of any link, information, or opportunity contained in this book or within any other information disclosed by the Author or the Publisher in any form whatsoever.

YOU SHOULD ALWAYS CONDUCT YOUR OWN INVESTIGATION (PERFORM DUE DILIGENCE)
BEFORE BUYING PRODUCTS OR SERVICES FROM ANYONE. THIS INCLUDES PRODUCTS AND SERVICES
SOLD VIA WEBSITE LINKS REFERENCED IN THIS BOOK.

www.ingramcontent.com/pod-product-compliance
Lightning Source LLC
Chambersburg PA
CBHW060515300426
44112CB00017B/2685